Far Beyond the Field

a story of lessons learned, guidance, hope, and encouragement ...

By Steven Frusolone

... and strength ... leadership ...
respect ... integrity ...
sportsmanship ... ethics ...
faith ... love ... family ...

... because the end of the game
is just the beginning.

Far Beyond the Field

Printed in the United States of America

Email your thoughts to:

info@FarBeyondtheField.com

ISBN: 978-0-615-21741-3

ACKNOWLEDGMENTS

This book is dedicated to the following:

To my wife, Diane, who is my best friend, my strength, my balance, and the love of my life.

To my children, Christian and Juliana, who I live for and who have taught me more about life than I could have ever possibly imagined.

To my mother, Connie, who was responsible for the change.

To my father, Anthony, who I never got the chance to know.

To my students and players, for giving me the opportunity to teach.

To the parents of my students and players, for your patience and kind words.

To all of those who have chosen to read this book. I hope that at least one thing in this book hits home.

FOREWORD

"She's gone." Those two words on April 12th, 2001, changed my life forever. Mere weeks prior to those two words and several years after those two words continue to impact me on every level. The realization of what happened that day changed my thoughts, my dreams, my aspirations, my parenting, my coaching, and my message for the rest of my life.

****

This book is not an autobiography, however, you'll find that the first few chapters deal with my life because I feel it is important for you to understand what is behind the message that I hope to convey in this book. It is a story about hope, encouragement, expectations, and priorities. My commitment to you, the reader, is to share some of the things I have learned as a son, a husband, a father, a coach, and a friend so that you can grow to apply these valuable lessons to your own relationships. I am confident that you will come away with a clear appreciation of some values that we must keep in mind with regards to today's children.

Chapter One

OKAY TO LET GO

As I stood at her bedside that brisk April day, she didn't look any different than she had the past two weeks. For fourteen days her body had been trapped inside a coma—only the machines looming behind her hospital bed kept her weak body alive. My hope was that she'd wake up and everything would be okay. My sense of reality told me otherwise. On April 12th, 2001, at the age of seventy-two, my mother, Connie, died of colon cancer that had spread throughout her body over a five-year period. And that's when I realized that her journey was finally over ... *and mine was just beginning.*

At the time of her diagnosis in 1996, after several operations, doctors gave her three to six months to live. I knew better than that. Not my mother; not a chance. You could never make my mother do something she did not want to do. She was, by far, the most stubborn woman I have ever met. One would never find my mother seeking refuge in the doctor's office. No, instead she battled and battled and refused to surrender to this illness, at least on the outside. I don't know what it was doing to her on the inside, because she would never let us in. But every Christmas Eve throughout those five years as the cancer ate away at her, she would somehow muster up the strength to host her traditional Italian Christmas Eve dinner.

The kitchen would be sizzling with her cooked Shrimp De'Johnge, gravy with calamari (calamod ... as us Italians say), fried smelts, shrimp cocktail, and of course, Dad's Root Beer. This was the same Christmas Eve dinner I have enjoyed my entire life. To this day, we continue the tradition.

Looking back on that month of April, we could never quite figure out what she was holding onto during those last two weeks in the hospital. My mother had made peace with the people she needed to make peace with, gave instructions to the people she yearned to instruct, and had accepted the fact that this disease had finally beaten her. We did not want my grandmother Irene, my mother's mother, to see her in the state she was in. As a father, I cannot possibly begin to imagine what it would be like to bury your own child. But the night before my mother passed, we decided to let my grandmother talk to her on the phone. Keep in mind that my mother was in a coma at this time. My brother and I were in the room and we held the phone up to my mother's ear as we heard my grandmother saying, "It's okay, Connie. You can let go now."

As my grandmother reassured her own daughter for the very last time, a tear spilled from my mom's right eye. With her head tilted slightly to the right, I watched that tear drizzle down her cheek, finding its way to her fragile jaw. My brother and I looked at each other in stunned silence. A wave of sadness yet relief flooded me; that teardrop confirmed what medical professionals had been saying for years. People have an awareness when they are in a coma. It also validated for me, personally, that there is a higher presence.

Very early the next morning, sometime around 2:30 AM, before she passed, she woke up from the coma. I guess "woke up" is a relative term in this sense. What I mean is that she sat up and opened her eyes. My brother and I had been sitting at her bedside around the clock for two straight days and we were there when she sat up in bed that morning. I will never forget the look on her face. It was a surreal expression of fear, anxiety, helplessness, and love all bundled together. With my brother on one side of her and myself on the other, she clutched our hands as tight as could be, releasing any remaining fear in her firm squeeze. This lasted about two minutes or so. She couldn't speak, but she didn't need to. She slowly loosened her hands from ours, laid back down, and went back into the coma.

Later that morning, around 9:30, my brother and I left the room to get a cup of coffee at the hospital cafeteria. We weren't gone more than twenty minutes. My mother, and I'm sure she planned it this way, passed away while we were gone.

****

Mom and I were never that close, yet we shared this strange trust that got broken and repaired over and over again. She learned to accept the hand that God had dealt her in life. My childhood was tough, but I can't even begin to fathom how much more difficult hers was. But those heart-wrenching final weeks of her life have brought me to this point in my own existence where I now love better, learn better, teach better, and hopefully have just become a better human being.

My mom worked several jobs throughout her life. In her younger days, she worked for a doctor's office. This ultimately played a large role in her life because I remember her telling me that a doctor she worked for once warned her, "Stay away from doctors. They will kill you." Well, my mom certainly heeded those words and stayed away from doctors. The only time she would ever go was if we needed to rush her to the emergency room for something. That happened on several occasions. The most memorable time being when a tumor the size of a grapefruit was detected growing inside of her. This was the start of an agonizing five-year period for me, but more so for her.

Other jobs she had through the years included running the books for my stepfather's business, working in grocery stores, and managing a fast-food restaurant. One of *my* favorite jobs that she had was managing an Italian bakery on the far northwest side of Chicago. I learned very quickly what a fresh bakery does with unsold items at the end of the day.

In retrospect, she was the absolute best cook I've ever known. Times were certainly different back then. She cooked from scratch, with real butter, plenty of salt, and lots of oil. She once said that if leftovers didn't have a layer of grease on top the next day then it wasn't made properly. She very rarely used recipes so it was nearly impossible to recreate her meals. To this day, we try, but still can't get things right, probably due to a lack of butter and oil.

She was, at times, the most generous person you could ever come across. Those rare times that Mom had money to spend, she'd always end up buying something nice for someone else. That's the kind of person she was. I don't think I'll ever fully understand some of the decisions that she made and to be honest, I've quit trying. Deep in my heart I know there are some dark secrets in her past but I've never been able to unearth them. I loved her dearly, but I'm sure that I never showed it, at least to her anyway. In the end though, during those last two weeks she was in the hospital, I was at her side every single day. I'll never know if Mom knew I was there when she sat up in bed and awoke from her coma the morning that she passed, but for my peace of mind I truly hope she did know.

Chapter Two

NOT YOUR BIG ITALIAN FAMILY

I was born in Chicago, Illinois, at Presbyterian St. Luke's Hospital in 1965. My brother, Robert, my only sibling, is four and a half years older than me. For the first year of my life, we lived on Ashland Avenue just off of Taylor Street, a neighborhood heavily populated with feisty Italians. Over the years, we moved several times, once to the west side of Chicago and a couple of times to Elmwood Park. I attended Our Lady Help of Christian's School through third grade in Chicago, Elm Elementary School in Elmwood Park from fourth through eighth grade, and finally Holy Cross High School in River Grove. Holy Cross was an all boys Catholic school, with our sister school, Mother Theodore Guerin, right across the parking lot. Holy Cross and Mother Guerin have since merged and now go by the name of Guerin Prep.

Baseball was a part of my life from very early on. As a young child, when I was probably five or six years old, I used to sit on the back porch of our bungalow, located on Long Avenue between Division Street and Augusta Boulevard with my grandfather, Nunzio, and watch Cubs games. He would sit at the end of a futon looking couch and I would lay my head on his lap and watch the game in comfort. More often than not, this ended up being my afternoon nap. Years later, my grandmother Irene confessed to me that Grandpa used that time for his afternoon naps as well. This startling revelation did not spoil the beautiful memories I have of those carefree summer afternoons. My love of baseball is probably the reason why I've come to cherish those once-in-a-lifetime moments I spent at my grandfather's side.

Things were so different back then. In those days, kids lived to play baseball. Today it is rare to find a baseball field occupied on a summer day. In the evenings, fields are filled with various organized youth leagues. Modern-day statistics reveal that 97 percent or more of children today do not play baseball beyond the age of fourteen. I will elaborate more on that later.

For now let's just say that I belong in the remaining 3 percent bracket.

My grandfather died from a heart attack on my seventh birthday which was April 7th, 1972. Suddenly the days of watching baseball with Grandpa were long gone. I clearly remember the strength my grandmother showed after losing the man she had spent her entire life with. We were sitting on the front steps of our bungalow in Chicago the day after Grandpa had passed away and she was calmly explaining to me that he was up in heaven with God. I looked deep into her eyes full of wisdom and saw that they were completely dry. Despite her pain, she didn't shed a single tear, at least not in front of me.

My grandmother forged ahead for years. In August of 2005 at the age of ninety-eight, my grandmother left this world to join the man she loved. Thinking back, she and my mother were two of the strongest women I have ever known. But out of the two, my grandmother was the stronger one. Not only was Gram, as we used to call her, as tough as leather, she was also one of the healthiest women I ever had the good fortune of knowing. She never smoked or drove a car. She only consumed alcohol on Christmas and that was usually limited to one drink or so. There's no denying that this woman had a tough life, but that is a novel in itself. If you let her, and that was quite easy to do, she would tell you stories that would astound you. Her one true vise in life was God.

My grandfather worked for the City of Chicago in the Streets and Sanitation Department. To say he knew many people would be an understatement. The most famous of his acquaintances was probably Al Capone, the notorious Chicago mobster. The fact that my grandfather knew him also meant my grandmother had the chance to meet him as well. From what I understand, she once cooked for him. During the last couple of years of my grandmother's life, my brother and I encouraged her to write her memoirs. In my opinion, that would have been a real page-turner.

As I mentioned before, my grandmother lived a wearisome life. Born in Bari, Italy, in 1906, she came to the United States around 1912 by boat. In the year 1925, she married Chicago resident Nunzio Prete.

Throughout her entire life, she had to endure controversy, gambling, alcoholism and the deaths of her daughter, brother and sister, close friends, and other people she cared for. Be that as it may, she somehow always maintained her faith in God to carry her through. I once gave her a framed picture (a pretty popular one) of footprints in the sand. I don't exactly remember the wording inscribed on it, but if my memory serves me correctly it had something to do with two sets of footprints leading up to just one set during harrowing times. The premise was that the solitary set of footprints belonged to God who in reality was carrying us through some of the most difficult times in life. My grandmother always used to refer to that picture and tell me how true it was. Up until the time of her death, my grandmother was a devout Catholic woman.

Irene, as her friends called her, was truly an amazing woman. Ask anyone who ever knew her and they will tell you the same. One of the things I admired most about her is that she was far younger than her years. Up until the last few years of her life, she was healthier than all of us. Instead of taking it easy during her golden years, my grandmother held a job up until she was eighty-eight years old. I remember a great story she once told me about her last job as a floor and stock clerk at Sears. She had to contend with two different bosses in the few years that she worked there. The first thought she was only sixty years old when, in fact, she was twenty years older. The second, according to my grandmother was quite a piece of work. Irene used to tell this story about how he wanted her, an eighty-eight-year-old woman, to climb up about ten or twelve stairs on a ladder and get a box off the top shelf. She looked him squarely in the eye and said, "Would you send *your* grandmother up there to do that?" Needless to say, she stopped working for Sears shortly after.

My life with my father ended before it really had a chance to begin. Anthony Frusolone was born on July 11th, 1925 in Chicago, Illinois. In 1969, he was diagnosed with Multiple Sclerosis at the age of forty-four. He passed away on October 12th, 1975. I was only ten years old at the time and he had been in a long-term care facility for five years prior to his death. Multiple Sclerosis is a horrible disease of the central nervous system and can be broken down into four categories. My father had Primary Progressive MS, which is the most severe form of the disease. Even though she tried, my mother could not provide the care he needed as his disease worsened. We would visit him on Sundays at the long-term care facility in Oak Lawn, Illinois, quite far from where we lived.

I have very few memories of my father. One of the things I do remember about him was his five o'clock shadow and how it used to scratch my face when I hugged him hello or goodbye. I also recall my brother and I shooting pool in the visitor's recreation room every time we'd pay him a visit at the long-term care facility he was forced to call home. But sadly, I do not have a single significant memory of my father living with us or him standing on his own two feet. No matter how hard I try, I can't seem to remember ever having had a meaningful conversation with him. This is an extremely empty void in my life that I wish I could fill. The need to understand more about our relationship continues to eat away at me. Was there ever a relationship to speak of? Did he love me? These are the questions that I keep wrestling with from time to time. I'm sure he loved me. I can't even begin to realize how difficult things must have been for him. It must have really torn him apart back then knowing that we couldn't have the type of relationship that a father and son should have. To this day, it still tears me apart. I miss him terribly and I didn't even know him.

I guess I didn't know any better at the time, but as I reflected on things years later, many unanswered questions came to mind. For starters, I wondered why he was living in a facility so far away. Why didn't we visit him more often? Why was my mother remarrying during the latter years of my father's illness? Where was my father's side of the family throughout this whole terrible ordeal?

After my mother passed away, I kept having this disturbing recurring dream where I would wake up in tears so angry at her for not letting me be a bigger part of my father's life and keeping me from getting to know him. What kind of father was he? What was he like? I'd give anything to hear the answer to these questions.

I have a couple of photographs of my father taken during his days in the Navy. He served during World War II on a Patrol Torpedo Boat (PT 321) as a Gunner's Mate operating in the South Pacific in 1943 and 1944. Unfortunately, that is really the extent of the details that I am aware of. About the only remnants that we have are the old Navy photographs that I've mentioned. My aunt was gracious enough to pass them on to us.

After my mother had remarried, my mother and stepfather's house burned down in 1996 and we lost ninety-five percent of our personal belongings. The fire department determined that raccoons had chewed through some exposed wires up in the attic and this is what caused the fire. The biggest loss, in addition to my baseball card collection that probably would have been worth a couple hundred thousand dollars by now, was the photographs of the man who fathered me. As a way to cope with my traumatic childhood, I have suppressed so many memories. I desperately needed those photographs and still do. Without them, I have little way of keeping my father's memory alive.

Ironically, and you'll figure out why it was ironic later, one of the things that did survive the fire in 1996 was all of my *plastic* baseball trophies. I am certainly thankful that they did.

One of the things I do know about my father was that at one time he was a sales manager at a car dealership in Chicago. Supposedly his partner wanted to start using hard rubber on the inside of cars for the dashboard, arm rests, etc. My father didn't think there was a future in that idea. From what I understand, his partner went on to become a multi-millionaire with this idea. So I guess it's safe to say my father was not the risk taker that his youngest son turned out to be.

My brother, Robert, is perhaps the smartest man I know. He is a former Naval Intelligence Officer and once entertained job opportunities with the FBI and CIA. Like many of us, he ended up settling for a career in Corporate America. I say this because I believe he is far too special a person to have to fight trying to get ahead in Corporate America. I love him and his family to death, but as the years have gone by and our families have grown, we just do not see enough of each other. We let ourselves get caught up in our daily lives and just don't plan accordingly. Actually, I am the one to blame for us having grown apart. But the guilt that I feel does not diminish my love for him and I hope he realizes this.

Chapter Three

BASEBALL, THE EARLY YEARS

One of the hardest things for me to deal with throughout the years has been the loss of my father. It wasn't until nearly twenty years after his passing that I realized just how much I missed having a father around. That is probably the reason why I am so close to my kids now. I didn't have a father to take walks with or play catch with. There was no father figure around to coach my team, or mentor me. My mother was all those things for me. But, I had far too much freedom as a kid. As a result of it, I made some awfully bad choices at times. Somehow I managed to come away relatively unscathed. That is how things were back then. We were much more "street smart" than kids are today.

While my mother took on the role of both mother and father for my brother and I, my grandmother really did play an active role in our upbringing. My mother worked a full time job and my grandmother was who would watch us. She lived with us so it certainly made it easier on my mother. I do have this one enduring memory of my mother and me playing catch on the sidewalk in front of our house in Chicago. I believe I was in third grade. The mailman would walk by and my mother would always tell him, "My son is gonna be a star someday." Well, I never quite achieved that star status my mother dreamed of, but I did have a pretty long and successful (in my opinion) career in baseball.

When my mother passed away in 2001, I was thirty-six years old and still playing baseball in a men's league. It was a league comprised of players who were twenty-eight years old and up. Believe it or not, it was quite competitive. The league consisted of many ex-college players and some minor leaguers. Pitchers would typically throw anywhere from seventy to eighty miles per hour. At my mother's funeral during the eulogy, several people got up to say something about her. I could not bring myself to do it, but I did have my brother-in-law read what I had written. It basically related the story of us playing catch and the comments she used to tell the mailman. The brief note to my mom ended by saying, "I'm sure you'll be pleased to know that I'm still, at the age of thirty-six, playing baseball on a semi-professional level. I may not have become the star you fantasized about, but I want you to know that you're my own bright shining star looking down on me from heaven."

While a couple of bad decisions no doubt affected how far I could have gone as a baseball player, it sure didn't stop me from trying. The first part of my Little League career ended as quickly as it began. I was in the third grade. I was playing in a league on the northwest side of the city of Chicago and the bulk of our games were played at Amundsen Park. As I mentioned earlier, I have suppressed so many of my childhood memories, so you'll have to forgive me for not remembering what team I was on. In my first game, I came face-to-face with a hard throwing left-handed pitcher. The very first pitch was a laser beam that caught me square on my left knee. I remember trying to tough it out ... but just couldn't do it. I left the game crying and never returned that season.

When that school season ended in 1973, we moved from Chicago out to the "suburbs" in Elmwood Park. At the time, it seemed like miles and miles away. Not until I started driving in 1981 did I realize that it was only about a fifteen minute drive. To satisfy my gnawing curiosity, recently I actually looked it up on the Internet and was surprised to see it was less than ten miles away, but yet a world apart. The neighborhood we had moved from had really changed. Let's just say, it was no longer a neighborhood where kids could play outside until the street lights came on. I had my bike stolen at knifepoint. My stepfather owned a service station on Division Street, just east of Austin Blvd. Several times, including once with my brother present, they were robbed at gunpoint.

Elmwood Park, on the other hand, was a very nice neighborhood made up of pricey homes. The town had a heavy Italian influence. Two doors away from us lived an alleged mobster with a black iron gate surrounding his house. He used to give me and a friend of mine $100 to help unload the truckload full of fireworks he used to receive every Fourth of July. He would hand me the money and say, "Don't tell your mother, kid." We learned very quickly how to get a $100 bill cashed; we'd go to the pharmacy and buy candy or baseball cards. It was a pretty sweet deal.

The summer of 1973 when we moved to Elmwood Park, I was a bit of a shy kid and really didn't make any new friends right away. I ballooned up to 110 pounds in fourth grade. It was my first year in a new school and a new neighborhood. My situation changed one beautiful October day. We lived less than two blocks from school and my mother used to come to school and walk me home. One day, while walking home, there was a boy casually strolling along in front of us. I said to my mom, "That boy is in my class." So what did my mom do? She asked the boy point-blank, "Will you play with my son?" I was so embarrassed that my face must have turned beet red. But much to my surprise, the boy said yes! That boy's name was George Salerno, and he went on to become my best friend for years and years. His family owned Salerno Funeral Home. As George became an adult, he eventually took over the family business. Ironically, George buried my mother in 2001.

George and I were inseparable that winter. As the spring of 1974 rolled around, we, like all kids, would get out our baseball gloves and play catch. I was still a pudgy fourth grader, but I sure could throw a baseball. One day, we were playing catch at the school playground when George's dad, George Sr., pulled up in his black Lincoln Continental. George Jr. was extremely excited to have his dad see how far I could throw. George's dad was head coach of one of the Little League baseball teams in Elmwood Park. One phone call later and I became the newest member of his team. I was determined to get back to playing baseball after that devastating (traumatic to me anyway) pitch the previous year in Chicago.

Little League baseball was a big thing in Elmwood Park. It was back in the day when there was an Opening Day Parade. That was pretty cool. All the kids would get dressed up in their uniforms, take team pictures, and march in the parade. Shortly after that, the games would start. Our team, the Phillies, had to wear black itchy nylon shirts and pants with white and black stirrup socks. But we couldn't care less. I'll never forget how proud I was to put on a uniform that day for that first game in Elmwood Park.

Our first game was played at Elmwood School. Yours truly was selected as the starting pitcher. I had never pitched before in my life, but my coach figured I must be able to pitch because I had a strong arm. And boy did I ever pitch! Much to everyone's surprise, I pitched a 12-0 shutout, and a no-hitter to boot. Not only that, but I hit a home run over the flags! We did not have a fence in the outfield at Elmwood School. They used to set up rope flags for the outfield fence. I got the game ball that day and it would end up being the first of many I received throughout my Little League career. The funniest thing about the home run is that it was one of only two that I hit over a fence (or flags) in my entire life. The even stranger part is, I hit the first one in my first game and the last one in my last game as an adult!

Chapter Four

THE ESCAPE

As I said earlier, I had a pretty tough childhood. For years, my family endured deaths, alcoholism and financial difficulty. The one thing I always had as my escape was sports. I heavily relied on baseball, basketball, football and hockey to help get me through the worst of times. As a youth, I never participated in organized football or hockey, but we used to play regularly during those seasons. I played Little League baseball and park district basketball from fourth through eighth grade. I also played basketball on our school team, the Elm Knights, from sixth through eighth grade. Back then, you actually had to try out for the team. Not everyone made it. That has certainly changed. After my first year of playing baseball, it seemed like I had finally been accepted and found myself hanging out with the "cool" kids. As strange and sad as it may seem, the good athletes were always considered the "cool" kids and given preferential treatment. Some things never change.

Although I'm ashamed to admit it, I was quite a plump fourth grader. Then again I had several strikes against me. We had just moved to a new town and I didn't have any friends to speak of. As I started to make more friends and play sports, I began to thin out. In fifth and sixth grade, I evolved into a good athlete.

Baseball was a huge part of our lives in our neighborhood throughout the summer. Sometimes I think it was the only thing that kept my sanity intact. We would be at the baseball field from nine o'clock in the morning until dinner time, rarely, if ever, stopping for lunch. If you were lucky enough, you also had a Little League game that night. Nobody had to make any calls to arrange a game. We all just showed up by instinct. On any given day, there would be ten to twenty kids roaming all over the field. We would play a game called lob league, which was basically a regular baseball game except that the ball would be pitched slowly. On the rare occasions where we did not have enough players for all the positions, we would do without a right fielder. It was an automatic out if you hit it to right field. Sometimes if there weren't enough players, we would skip having a first baseman and play pitcher's hand. Basically what that meant was that on a ground ball, instead of the fielder throwing to first, he would throw to the pitcher. If the ball got to the pitcher before you reached first base, you were out. We rarely ever used a catcher.

There were also times when we would only have two to four kids available to play. We would then play a game called fast pitching. It was played with a rubber ball and a box or strike zone taped to the brick school wall. The game was pretty self-explanatory from a ball and strike standpoint. Ground balls to a fielder meant that all he had to do was field it cleanly and throw it back to the pitcher for an out. A ground ball back to the pitcher and he in turn had to hurl the ball straight into the box on the wall for an out. A one hopper to the fence and it was a double, unless the fielder could throw it from the fence into the box on the wall. A triple had to hit the fence on a fly. You could also be thrown out on that too. Obviously, a ball over the fence was a home run. The greatest thing about that game was the variety of pitches you could throw with a rubber ball. Massive curve balls, split finger fast balls, screw balls, knucklers ... you name it. We had one kid who could throw a curve ball that would easily break four feet. I used to play this same game by myself sometimes when I couldn't find anyone around.

I was an incurable baseball fanatic. One winter I thought of another game I could play in my living room. With a Styrofoam ball and one of those small wooden bats they used to hand out every once in while at Chicago Cubs games, I would toss the ball up and hit it. The outcome solely depended on where it made contact in the living room. If the ball hit the ceiling or turned out to be a ground ball, it was an out. A line drive was a base hit pure and simple. If it hit high on the wall then it was a double. There were no triples, aside for one exception. If I hit the ball into the foyer on a fly, it counted as a home run. The exception to the triple rule was if a fast runner hit a double. How did I know it was a fast runner? Let's just say this was one detailed game. I used to always play my two favorite teams against each other; the Cubs versus the Philadelphia Phillies, my first Little League team. I knew both lineups by heart and used to keep a scorebook of these games. Mike Schmidt of the Phillies was my absolute favorite player.

Back in those days, we didn't have video games to keep us entertained. We didn't have the Internet either. I don't even think we owned a computer. We didn't have regular scooters, much less shiny electric ones. In lieu of motorized transportation, we rode our bikes or walked everywhere. Playing sports was the only real outlet available to us so we played them all the time. Bad weather didn't even stop us from doing so. We all had gloves with the ends of the fingers chopped off to allow us to throw a football or shoot a basketball. If it was too cold or rainy we simply played indoors. Hand hockey was always one of my favorites. The game was played on your knees and your hand was actually the hockey stick. The object of the game was to score a goal by slapping a Styrofoam ball into the designated net. In my house, the opening to the foyer was one goal and the fireplace opening the opposing one. This was a brutal game. Your knees would be so rug burned that you could barely walk afterward. It was also a very physical game, as fighting in hockey back then and even today was not only accepted, but expected.

During football season, we would play the game for hours. For us, there was no such thing as a game of two hand touch in football. We were tougher than the pigskin, I guess. Only tackle football seemed to satisfy us. We had no need for equipment either. If you didn't want to play tackle, you were out of luck.

When basketball and hockey season came around, our attention shifted toward playing these games. I invented a similar basketball game similar to my Styrofoam baseball game that could also be played indoors. I rigged up a Nerf™ net on my closet door in my bedroom for the purpose of playing full games just like I did with the baseball game. I even kept stats meticulously. My teams were always my two favorites, the Philadelphia 76ers because they had Julius Erving, better known as Dr. J., and my hometown Chicago Bulls. As long as I live, I'll never forget the time I was playing a game against a friend of mine. When I went up for a dunk, he went up to block it. Foul! Whoa, foul and broken window. We crashed right through my bedroom window. This was one of about twenty windows I had broken at my house playing sports.

I'm not implying we were all that different from the kids of today. These days, kids have far more distractions than we ever did. What I am saying is that I believe we turned out to be different people and sports played a major role in that. I also think we learned discipline the hard way. Nothing was handed down to us on a silver platter. If we wanted something, we had to work hard for it. There was no such thing as equal playing time. Adults were always brutally honest with us and they treated us fairly. We respected our coaches because they commanded it. The bottom line is we exercised more and used our imagination more. To fight boredom, we tapped into our creative juices and invented games.

Today's lack of creativity really concerns me. I strongly believe that a lack of imagination eventually leads to no innovation. Just take a look at our country's trade deficit. I can't help but wonder if the U.S. relies too heavily on other countries to be innovative for us.

****

Some time ago, I received a pretty funny and thought-provoking e-mail, one that talked about how things were different for kids who grew up in the 50's, 60's and 70's. It mentioned several things:

First, we survived being born to mothers who smoked and/or drank alcohol while they were pregnant. They took aspirin, ate blue cheese dressing, tuna from a can and didn't get tested for diabetes.

We were put to sleep on our tummies in our baby cribs. We wore bright colored pajamas and were covered under bright colored blankets, all loaded with lead based paints.

We had no childproof lids on medicine bottles, doors or cabinets and when we rode our bikes, we had no helmets.

As infants and children, we would ride in cars with no car seats, booster seats, seat belts or air bags.

Riding in the back of a pickup truck on a warm day was always a special treat.

We drank water from the garden hose. We shared one soft drink with four friends from the same can or bottle and nobody actually died from this.

We ate cupcakes, white bread and real butter. We drank sodas and Kool-Aid loaded with sugar but we weren't overweight because we were always outside playing. We would leave home in the morning and play all day as long as we were back home by the time the streetlights came on. We didn't have cell phones so the only way for our parents to reach us was to drive around the neighborhood and find us. And we were OK.

We would spend hours building go-carts out of scraps and then ride down the hill, only to find out that we forgot to put brakes on the go-cart. After running into the bushes, curbs and trees a few times, we learned how to solve the problem.

We did not have Playstation™, Nintendo™ or X-Box™. We had about five or six channels of television to watch, not more than a hundred like today. We did not have DVD's, CD's, Ipod's™, PC's, the Internet, text messaging or chat rooms. We had friends and went outside to play with them.

We fell out of trees, got cut, broke bones and lost teeth and there were no lawsuits filed because of these accidents. Our coaches yelled at us and our parents did not complain.

We ate worms and mud pies made from dirt. The worms did not live inside us forever. We swallowed gum.

We were given BB guns for our 10th birthdays and we used sticks as swords. Although we were told it would happen, we did not put out very many eyes.

Little League had tryouts and not everyone made the team. Those who did not had to learn to deal with disappointment.

The idea of a parent bailing us out if we broke the law was unheard of. They actually sided with the law!

Looking back, we sure had it all ... freedom, failure, success and responsibility.

****

While I'm not advocating all of the things we did, my point is we were creative and innovative youngsters and we experienced life to the fullest. It was a pretty good deal for us. It was especially beneficial for our health. Many experts believe that today's lack of creativity is causing many of the modern-day health problems. But it isn't necessarily the kids fault.

A recently released study in 2006 by the National Association for Sport and Physical Education and the American Heart Association suggest that most states receive a failing grade on their physical education requirements. This is eye-opening considering today's skyrocketing childhood obesity rates. In our country, we have approximately 30 percent of the states that do not mandate physical education for elementary and middle school students. The study also found that almost one-fourth of the states allow required Physical Education credits to be earned through online P.E. courses. Twelve states allow this! Can you believe it? Is PlayStation™ one of these so called courses? The figures in this report known as the Shape of the Nation Report will amaze you.

This, to me, emphasizes the need for us, as parents and coaches to stay involved. We need to offer our kids the opportunity to participate in physical activities and instill in them that a little bit of competition can be healthy. Parents should encourage their children to exercise more and become active in sports. However, in doing so, we also need to make sure our child's sports experience is a positive one. This is one way to build their confidence. It is also our responsibility to teach them about respect, integrity, sportsmanship and ethics. But no matter how much we want them to, we should never try to force our children to participate in activities or sports they dislike. The only thing we can do is encourage them and hope that it will have an impact in their lives.

As much as I hate to admit it, I am far harder on my own children than on any of the other kids that I coach. There is a reason why I expect more out of them. I want them to strive for excellence in everything they do. Whether it is in sports, playing the piano or acting in the school play, I want them to feel passionate about what they are doing. I know they won't achieve excellence all of the time. That's not really the point. I am hard on them so that they understand I want them to try to reach their full potential. Back in my day, we didn't have the opportunities kids have today. In my opinion, our coaches were not as knowledgeable as they are in this day and age. Everything was so simple back then. We didn't have our swings or shooting motions broken down on video for us to learn from our mistakes. I can only imagine how much better of an athlete I might have been had I ever actually received any instruction. We got by on raw talent back then.

I want to be crystal clear about something. While I am harder on my own children than others, my kids play sports because they enjoy them. But they are also strongly encouraged by my wife and I to do so. Our thoughts are twofold. First, we both feel, adults and children alike, learn a lot about life, teamwork, hard work, sportsmanship, social skills and other things by participating in sports. Second, we believe that by staying active, our children are not only contributing to a healthy lifestyle, but are also less likely to become involved in unhealthy outside activities that might not be good for hem. Of course, their school activities take precedence over any and all sport activities in our house.

I do believe sports are important to children for a variety of reasons. In addition to teaching them physical fundamentals, I think, more importantly, that sports teach some of the character building life skills that I mentioned above. I also believe that one trait that we learn through sports really stands out ... disappointment. How children handle disappointment can go a long way into the overall character of the person they become. Our job, as parents and coaches is to support the children. So how do we do this? We talk to them about it. In particular, I believe there are four key things that we should discuss with them.

Personally, I try to discuss these things with my children before the disappointments occur.

The first area is acceptance. If you don't accept failure, how can you succeed? What will drive you? Baseball is a game of failure. For example, if you get three hits in every ten at-bats in baseball, that is a .300 batting average. If you do that your entire life, do you know where you'd end up? In the Hall of Fame! Pitching is similar. All you have to do is throw strikes 50 percent of the time and you will be a highly successful pitcher.

The next thing I talk to them about is staying positive. I tell them to reflect back on the things that went well for them. What made those things work well for them? Was it the preparation? Was it the energy they had that day? Why were they so focused?

Third, I try to teach them how important adjustments are to make. This certainly varies by sport. One of my goals as a coach is to get them to understand how important it is to make adjustments in the areas in which they weren't as successful as they wanted to be. How much did it bother them that they couldn't adjust to the given scenario? How will they handle it next time?

The last thing I try to get across to them is how to cope with disappointment and controlling their emotions. This is often the most difficult thing for them to do. Tempering their emotions after a disappointing circumstance is one of the keys to overcoming it. The finest coaching move I've made to this day came when I was managing an eleven and twelve-year-old baseball team. We had, arguably, the best pitcher in the league that year. He was probably the best overall player in the entire league. Best from a talent perspective, that is. His attitude was not the greatest, nor how he handled himself during challenging situations. The other kids on the team really looked up to this boy. In one particular game, he had just struck out with the bases loaded in the last inning of a tie game. He did not handle himself well when he came back to the dugout. He was not scheduled to pitch at all in that game. Instead, I recognized the opportunity that I had in front of me. After thinking it over, I decided to put him in to pitch after that strikeout. I reminded the boy about how important it was for him to forget that at-bat and concentrate on the job in front of him. At the end of the season, I asked my players from that team to tell me one thing they learned that year. This particular player said he learned how to deal with his emotions in a game. A couple of years later, he said how much of an impact that one game had made on him. Once again, I will repeat, this goes far beyond sports.

I am certain that I am not the only coach or instructor who has a philosophy with regards to a teaching approach. It is vital for youth organizations to hold coaches to a high set of standards and to ensure that they are adhered to. Today, more than ever, parents and coaches have huge responsibilities to live up to. It is our duty to make sure young athletes enjoy positive experiences. It is our obligation to help kids understand where sports fit in our lives. Sports are a privilege, not a right. This is a sentiment I try to make all of my players, students and children understand. Sports are something we get to do when all the other things have already been done. In my house, we have a rule that if homework is not done, my children are not allowed to attend whatever sporting event interests them at the time. It does not matter to me how significant that particular game might be. Simple rule: sports are a privilege.

While there are plenty of athletic stars in the making out there, we have to realize, as parents and coaches, that more than 99 percent of the young athletes we are raising or coaching will not go on to a professional sports career.

But even staying involved and encouraging our kids to participate comes with a price tag. Our youth organizations, park district programs and travel teams all cost money and in some cases, quite a bit of it. As for attending professional sporting events, you better have plenty of cash. Back in the day we used to hop on the bus and travel down Addison Avenue to Wrigley Field to see the Cubs play. We could ride the bus, watch the game and eat for well under $20. I recently took my family to a Cubs game. The tally will amaze you. We had pretty good seats, but not the best. We didn't travel by bus. Instead, we drove and parked near the stadium. Of course the children got hungry so we ate. We bought my two kids each a sweatshirt. That afternoon excursion ended up costing me a whopping $300! Pro basketball games aren't any cheaper. What about a Chicago Bears game? That will cost you even more. Despite the mounting costs, we still go because I do not want my kids to miss out on the opportunities that I had growing up to see professional athletes. I believe the success experienced by some of the professional athletes I watched during my youth years fueled my desire to excel in athletics. In all honesty, I want my kids to be good in sports. What parent doesn't? But all in all, it is becoming less important to me.

We can all continue to teach many of the things that I have been discussing in a variety of fashions. Sports just happen to be a convenient delivery mechanism to achieve them.

Chapter Five

THE DECISION

After I graduated from elementary school in 1979, I, having my mother's blessing, decided to attend Holy Cross High School in River Grove, Illinois. This was not an easy decision for my mom to make. Holy Cross, at the time, was a very expensive private school. My brother had attended St. Pat's in Chicago.

I played baseball, basketball, and football in high school. Baseball by far was my best sport from an athletic standpoint. I probably worked harder in basketball because I couldn't stand the fact that I was not a starter. I kept trying to convince myself that if I worked harder than everyone else, I'd somehow get into the starting lineup. That never happened. What I didn't realize is working harder didn't make me taller and it didn't make me that much of a better shooter. It did make me a better defensive player though. Even to this day when I play pick-up basketball, I push myself to the limit on defense. I guess some old habits die hard. Back then I couldn't stomach it when a player scored on me and I still feel the same way.

Throughout my high school years there were several occurrences that had a deep impact on my life. My mother and stepfather were going through some very difficult times. They had lost the service station they owned in Chicago and were in the process of losing our home. Just as my grandmother turned to God in her time of need, my parents turned to a bottle of whiskey, scotch, vodka or whatever the flavor of the day might have been. It's odd, but it seems as though many people from my era grew up with alcoholism in their family. If you've never experienced that, you might not fully understand. If you have, then I'm sure we probably have some very similar stories. The shouting matches, the confrontations, both verbal and physical, the medical emergencies, not to mention the crying, all took its toll on me. I once had my stepfather put a gun in my face. Another time, in self-defense I knocked out his two front teeth with a punch when he came at me in a drunken rage.

All of these things led to some decisions that had to be made during my junior and senior years in high school. I quit playing basketball and football so I could work and help out financially at home. Much to my disappointment, I gave up the idea of going away to college. I was a promising baseball player but almost had to give up the game. Out of anger and disappointment, I developed this ridiculously bad attitude that ultimately probably cost me a chance at a college scholarship.

****

In the summer before my senior year, I played what was probably the most important game of my teenage years in American Legion baseball. It was one of the best times in my young life. We had a very talented group of kids on that team. Quite often, college scouts would be at our games. Sometimes, pro scouts would be there as well. The game that I describe below was one of those games that had both pro and college scouts in attendance. I had the opportunity before the game to talk to several of them. The best part was *they really were interested in speaking with me.*

I was having a terrific season as the starting shortstop for the team. I could play shortstop with the best of them. I had it all—range, the glove, a strong arm and most importantly baseball intelligence. Forgive me for bragging but I was nearly a five tool player which is exactly what scouts back then looked for. Granted, I may not have been a power hitter, but in my opinion, a great hitter with speed. I could drive the ball. That summer, I was absolutely hammering the ball. I batted usually second or fifth. This particular game, I was batting second.

I won't go into all of the details, but I will describe the seventh inning that changed my life completely. Unfortunately, it wasn't until recently that I realized how much it shaped my life. The game was played during our American Legion regional tournament.

It was the bottom of the seventh in a tie game. We found ourselves in a win and advance situation. If we lost, our season would be over, just like that. It was pretty dramatic stuff for a teenager. Picture this if you will. Our leadoff hitter doubles to the left. I am the next batter up. Now, keep in mind that I am batting something like .570 during this summer season. Determined, I step up to the plate and look to my third base coach for my sign. I'm on my own. Absolutely perfect! I'm thinking I am going to rip this first pitch curveball to the gap and win the game and in the process land a scholarship or get drafted into the major leagues and then live the good life. I was a fantastic first pitch fastball hitter and there was not a chance in hell this guy was going to throw me a first pitch fastball.

As expected, I get the curve. I take the hardest swing I have ever taken in my life. Forget the gapper to left center; I'm going yard. Pretty silly thought considering that the only ball I had ever hit over a fence (or flags) during a game was in my first Little League game ever. I foul the pitch straight back to the screen. It's okay though. I have faced this pitcher several times throughout my career. I know his habits like the back of my hand. My instincts tell me he is going to come back with the fastball. He knows perfectly well I was a mere two inches from taking his curveball out. He thinks I'm expecting another curveball so he's going to try to sneak a fastball past me.

I step out of the box, adjust my batting gloves and look to the third base coach for guidance. He gives me the sign. He gives me the friggin' sign. To my surprise, he calls for a sacrifice bunt to move the runner to third. The only better hitter than me on our team was our third batter who was on-deck. I'm being asked to move the runner over so our third batter can win the game. This rush of disappointment kills my enthusiasm in an instant. I step in the box and quickly ask the umpire for time. Not only do I have tears of anger in my eyes, but I am in no frame of mind to step back in that batter's box. Can you believe this? I say to myself for my own benefit, "I'm batting almost .600 in the most important at-bat of my life, and this guy calls for me to bunt."

As I step out of the box and fidget with my gloves and helmet, I glance over to third one more time. I am given the same sign. I can hardly believe my eyes.

Despite my anger and disappointment, I step back in the batter's box and wait for the fastball I know is coming. From the stretch, the pitcher delivers the fattest, juiciest fastball I've ever seen and I have to bunt! I'm not exactly sure when I made the decision that would impact me to this day, considering you have about a second between the time when the ball leaves the pitcher's hand to when it reaches the plate, but in the end I ignore the bunt sign and swing away. You should have seen it. It was probably the laziest looping liner one could ever see right at the bag at second. The second baseman catches it, steps on the bag, double play. Our next hitter, our best hitter, comes to the plate and rips a single to left. A single that would have scored the runner I was supposed to move over to third. We did not score that inning and ended up losing the game when the other team scored in the top of the eighth. Ironically, they scored on a double, *a sacrifice bunt* and a sacrifice fly. Well, maybe it isn't so ironic.

After I hit into the double play, not a soul in the dugout said a word to me. They all knew I had been given the bunt sign. The players, the coaches and most importantly to me, the scouts ALL knew I had the bunt sign. Anybody with any baseball sense at all knew I had the bunt sign.

After the game, one of the scouts did decide to speak to me. He said (and I'll never forget the look on his face), "very, very, very bad decision." I'm not saying I would have gotten drafted anyway, but any chance that I had went out the window because of my ridiculously selfish, poor attitude.

****

I think about the events of that day quite often. There is no turning back, obviously, but I hope to have made some adjustments in my life and the lives of others based on that experience. I have that memory, and several others, that I purposely remind myself of to hopefully help me be a better person.

That season ended but life continued on. Contrary to what I thought that evening, and pardon the cliché, but the sun did come up the next morning. What hadn't changed for quite awhile though was my attitude. I really didn't care. And that has often haunted me. It wasn't about the opportunity that I had in front of me. What made it so wrong that I didn't care about this was the fact that I completely disrespected my coaches, my teammates, the game, myself, and my parents. I was raised better than that. I was taught to respect people and show integrity. I was raised to show sportsmanship and good ethics. I was so selfish and was willing to put it all on the line for no good reason. At the time, I blamed my mother and stepfather. I blamed my dad who died when I was ten. I blamed my coaches for holding me back. I was determined to get back at all of the people in my life who told me I couldn't do something. I blamed everyone, except myself.

Chapter Six

ALL GROWN UP

I graduated from high school in the spring of 1983 following that fateful baseball game. During my senior year, I had been working part-time at Ace Hardware in Franklin Park, Illinois. The summer after I graduated I started working full-time in the electrical department to help pay the bills at home. My ex-teammates all went on to play fall ball. I did enroll at Triton College in River Grove, IL, although I was not sure why I had done so. Perhaps I thought it was what I was supposed to do. Whatever the true underlying reason was, I began studying Fire Science Technology.

Upon nearing completion of my college coursework, I took the fireman's test and passed. That was no easy feat as the test is an extremely physically and emotionally draining one. I served a very brief stint as a paid-on-call fireman in my town. I absolutely loved every minute of that job. Unfortunately, well actually fortunately, small suburban fire departments are not exactly flooded with calls about blazing infernos. Shortly before my second year in school, I also changed jobs. Convinced that I needed to start thinking seriously about a career, I got a job working at United Stationers in Forest Park, IL. I was hired on as an Inventory Control Clerk. Basically, I became a zombie. It was a cycle counter job and we worked from midnight until 8:30 AM. I would go from work straight to school and then come home and sleep for a few hours. Not sure if any of you have ever worked the "graveyard" shift, but I do not think that you ever really adjust to it. I was tired all the time.

I did try out for the baseball team at Triton College and I made the team as a walk-on. However, I quit that team too because I wasn't starting. Players who try out for and make a college sports team without a scholarship generally do not get to play. I can't say that is always the case, but I do know it happens quite often. But the reality is that I never even gave it a chance.

Good grief! What an attitude I had. I left school shortly after I quit baseball. Here I was, six hours away from a college degree, and I threw it all away because I wasn't able to play baseball. To this day, when I tell this story, people ask if I ever did or if I ever will go back and finish what I started. I can't say that I blame them. It's only logical that people will ask. Regrettably, I did not make up those six hours and to this day, I do not have a degree hanging on my wall. This is something I am not proud of.

I continued working at United Stationers for several years. Due to my determination to create a career for myself, I kept getting promoted and ultimately ended up working in what was then called MIS (Management Information Systems). Most people now know that as Information Technology or IT. A few years later, as part of what came to be known as Black Thursday, I was let go from United Stationers due to a workforce reduction, but with a career in IT ahead of me. Ironically, I rejoined the company some seventeen years later.

While I was working at United Stationers, I met Diane, the woman that I would ultimately end up marrying on September 2nd, 1990. We first lived in Elmwood Park, IL, before moving a couple of times and ending up in the far north suburbs of Chicago.

I bounced around jobs for a couple of years before deciding that I wanted to earn the big bucks and became an independent consultant. Basically, I was performing the same computer programming jobs that I had been, except now I was getting paid three times as much. I remember thinking at the time that I really made the right career choice. And it worked out that way for quite some time. The late 1990's and early 2000's saw great innovations and very high demand for qualified IT personnel.

In 1994, I formed a corporation and ran that business until the onset of off-shoring devastated the U.S. technology market in 2001. At that point, I decided it was time to go back to Corporate America and did so, with a Fortune 500 company outside Chicago.

The mid and late 1990's also brought the births of my two children, a beautiful, healthy boy and my precious little girl. Parenthood changes everything about you. It changes your priorities and how you think. It dictates the way you act. Most importantly, it shows you how to love in a way you didn't know existed. It cripples you when your kids get the flu. It makes you laugh, cry, cheer, yell, hurt, think, plan and smile; sometimes all in the same day. It creates a separate existence within you.

Take time to hug your kids every day and tell the people in your life that you love them.

But having children should not make you stop living your life. You need to have things, an escape, if you will.

From the time I was twenty, I continued to play sports, either 16-inch or 12-inch softball. I didn't quite hang up the spikes after my kids were born. Being a father did not stop me from playing in the men's twenty-eight and older league baseball. In fact, I still play quite a bit of 12-inch softball. Only I seem to enjoy what a privilege it is to play with much more purpose now that I'm older and wiser. I'm not sure if it has anything to do with that game back in 1982. More than likely, it has to do with the things I had come to realize since that unforgettable game. Not only do I enjoy playing more, but the memory that I am left with has defined who I am as a coach on the field, as a husband and father at home. Normally, I'm a fair guy, but I also believe in teaching the kids to work hard for the things they want. I do not allow them to walk on my baseball field or basketball court. I don't permit them to disrespect their coaches, teammates or even the opposing players they must face head-on. Under no circumstances do I let myself get conned into doing my kids' homework.

For the past several years that I've been coaching, one trend that has become common is the notion of equal playing time. That is a very interesting discussion because you can easily make a case for or against it. What is particularly interesting to me is how different it is today than when I was playing youth baseball in the 70's. I played shortstop, pitcher or catcher in nearly every game I ever played. Why? The reason is quite simple actually. I was one of the best players on the team. My dad was not the coach either. In today's youth athletics, you have several different options. There are in-house sports in which participation is typically limited by school boundaries. You have travel teams, which are sometimes not limited by boundaries. The big difference between travel teams and in-house teams is that players are usually selected by some sort of tryout. Travel sports are a much more competitive level of play. The concept is that the best athletes will try out for and make the travel teams. Travel sports are also extremely expensive as compared to in-house sports. In my town for example, our in-house baseball program costs $145. If you try out and are selected for a travel team, you can expect to pay somewhere between $1,000 and $1,500. The additional cost is made up of tournament entry fees, out of state trips, private instruction and more. Right, wrong or indifferent, quite often the youth travel athletes are the ones who go on to play high school sports.

Now, getting back to the concept of equal playing time, I have several opinions on this. I'll only share a few so that I don't bore you.

Learn how to deal with all of life's disappointments – there will be many.

My main complaint with equal playing time is that we really aren't teaching these kids to work hard for the proper reasons. Back in my day, you actually had to try out for our sixth grade basketball team. In my children's school, everyone who signs up to play basketball gets to play. Is that wrong? I would never say it is wrong to prevent someone from doing something they want to do. I also don't think that wrong is the proper term. I just think that at some point in their lives, these kids are not going to "make the team." Again, I am referencing sports but this applies to the real world. I do feel we need to start teaching our children that they have to work for the things they truly want. We just don't seem to breed any competition into these kids. It isn't that they aren't competitive; it's just that the competitiveness is relative to what is at stake. If there is little incentive to try hard, then kids won't see the point in doing so. Obviously this does not apply to all kids.

I do think it is important for kids to know that participation does not equal effort. The amount of effort somebody puts into something or everything, for that matter, speaks volumes about their character. If a student really puts forth extra effort in school, most likely he or she will put forth extra effort in life. Once we start to accept mediocrity as the norm, I believe we deny people the opportunity to achieve.

Maybe I am making too much of this, then again perhaps not. I have gotten to witness this firsthand. My son tried out for our town's travel 12U (twelve and under) baseball team. He made the first cut and actually had a very good tryout on the second and final day. After waiting a few days, we received the call that he did not make the team. He was the thirteenth pick on a twelve person team. I believe that I am very well-respected in my community. I could have pulled some strings to make sure he made the team. The bottom line was, I wanted my son to make the team because of his ability, not because of who his father was. I was not sure how he would handle the news as it was the first time that he ever had to try out to make a team. We had discussed this possibility before he decided to try out. The alternative if he did not make the team would be that he would still play in-house baseball. My son is a pretty laid back kid when it comes to sports and never really gets too high or low, which is a good thing. Sometimes I wish he would show more of that competitive fire that I think it takes to be successful.

When I told him he was not selected to the team, his first question to me was who did make the team. I rattled off the list of names. This was the first time that I saw a bit of fire from him with regards to baseball. In my opinion (and several other coaches and people who have seen him play), my son was a better player than several who did make the team. Several kids who did make the team knew it as well. My son knew it too. His fiery reaction was not what surprised me though. What surprised me the most were the words that came out of his mouth.

Christian: "So I worked hard, had a great tryout and still did not make the team. That's not fair."

Me: "You are right, that is not fair. But you really didn't put forth the effort leading up to the tryout that we had talked about, did you?"

Christian: "No, not really."

Me: "So what do you want to do about it?"

For the first time in his young baseball life, my son actually asked me to set him up on a hitting and pitching program so that he would have a better chance at making the travel team next year. You will find out more about this shortly, but for now let's just say that I am very involved with a youth baseball and softball academy. My son spends very little time there. You probably also know, if you are a parent, that it gets quite difficult to instruct your own child. That is probably why he doesn't spend much time with me at the academy. We are far too hard on our own children. That might be the reason why my wife sometimes does not allow me and my son to ride home together after a game.

Again, this is not about sports. Not being selected for the travel team hopefully will teach my son a couple of life lessons. I believe that it already has. I think that he now realizes there are different kinds of disappointment and I don't mean the "no more candy" kind. The other thing I hope he learned from this is that if you want something, you have to work at it. On the back end of this I hope he learns a third thing.

The following year, after working hard on his baseball skills, my son did make the travel team. And that, I believe, is the third lesson I wanted him to learn. Do not be a quitter. You can achieve something if you put in the effort.

Chapter Seven

TIME TO CHANGE

I never had a single opportunity to play catch with my father. This absolutely tears me apart when I think about it. He was either in a hospital or long-term care facility for the five years prior to his death. I was ten and really needed him. How I wish I could conjure up a memory of him standing on his own two feet or walking a short distance over to me. The truth is there isn't any recorded in my memory.

For years, I had these suppressed feelings that I didn't even know existed. I did not cry when my mother told me my father had passed away. I did not shed a single tear when I used to go see him in the long-term care facility every Sunday. In fact, I actually used to cry when my mom would order me to stop whatever I was doing and get ready to go see my dad. I did not cry at my father's wake or funeral. For that matter, I did not cry either when my grandfather, who I loved dearly, passed away on my seventh birthday. Not until late 2001, September to be exact, several months after my mother passed away, did I cry about any of these things.

I was angry on the inside for so many years. I'm sure that nobody ever noticed. How could they if I didn't even know it myself. To keep my mind off of these unpleasant things, I would go about my business, whether it was playing sports, working, being a husband or father. I'm not really one to self-diagnose my conditions, but deep-seated anger is the only thing I can figure would have prevented me from recalling these incredibly vital childhood memories.

So what was it that finally released my anger? To this day, I am not one 100 percent certain. I am, however, fairly confident that it was a combination of four things. Four very significant life-altering things.

The first was my mother's death in April of 2001. As I mentioned, our relationship was strained throughout the years primarily because of broken trust. I am not going to go into details anymore than I previously have in an earlier chapter because this is not about a crucifixion. This is about me learning to be a better person. I never spent time in my adult life talking to the woman who gave birth to me. Sure, I had weekly or monthly phone conversations with her, but I never really had a meaningful talk with her or truly listened to what she had to say. She had her flaws just like every other human being on this earth. But underneath her tough exterior, she was also a caring, loving person. She was dealt a very bad hand which she played to the best of her ability. Watching her suffer through near death operations, years of chemotherapy and radiation treatments, and ultimately coma and death has transformed me into a better person. I love my wife better. I love my children better. I treat people better. I am no longer nearly as selfish. I hope that I am a better human being.

****

It's okay to cry.

The next event that had a profound effect on me and hundreds and thousands, even millions of people, was the tragedy of September 11th, 2001. What transpired that day will remain embedded in our minds forever. I remember exactly where I was when I first heard the news. I was at work speaking with my wife on the phone. She was at home that day with my daughter who had not yet gone to preschool. She was giving me play-by-play commentary of what had happened. I remember her telling me that a plane flew straight into the World Trade Center. Right away I tried getting on CNN.com or any other news web site. They were all being flooded no doubt by millions of people trying to do the same thing. At that time, my wife, who was watching the breaking news on television, said, "Wait, they are showing it again. OH MY GOD! STEVE, IT'S ANOTHER PLANE! ANOTHER (expletive) PLANE JUST CRASHED INTO ANOTHER BUILDING!"

To this day, I still find myself watching shows about the events of 9/11. I don't know why, but maybe it is the sobering reminder about how quickly it can all be taken away from us. Maybe I watch them because I know for a fact that September 11th, 2001, changed me. It changed all of us. Hopefully, it made us all better people. I didn't cry on September 11th. I did go home and hug my children and my wife though. About a week or so after the tragedy, I was hitting golf balls at a driving range. The FAA up to that point had not allowed commercial airliners back in the air. There were a number of us at the driving range that day when the first airplane in more than a week flew overhead. EVERYONE stopped hitting balls at once and just stared up at the crystal blue sky as the plane slowly ascended. I'm not sure what triggered it, but my eyes filled with tears as a million thoughts flooded through my head.

I don't exactly remember when I cried but the important thing is that I did. I wept after having read stories of heroism. I cried when I heard songs that were written about the tragedy. I cried when professional baseball resumed play a few days after the tragedy and they sang God Bless America before the game. I broke down because I was hurting for all of the people affected by this. I cried because I was so angry and it made me feel better. The tragedy made me love my wife and children better than before. It also inspired me to treat people better. It made me not be so selfish. It has made me a better person.

****

The third event that I believe has changed my life is a bit complicated. My wife, like many others, does it all. She works part-time at a "job" but more than full-time at life. She takes on the role of mother, household CEO, chauffeur, coach and wife. In a nut shell she is Superwoman, at least in my eyes. You might think that we all do the same things. That is probably true. The difference is that people handle situations differently.

One early fall day in 2003, my wife called me from her cell phone and said she was being driven by a neighbor to the emergency room. She had severe pains in her stomach and side. I left work immediately and headed to meet her at the emergency room. From the emergency room check-in desk, I could hear her in pain. I was directed to the emergency room bay where she was. After some time, the pain finally subsided. They took her for X-rays, an ultrasound and, if I remember correctly, a CT Scan. The results confirmed what the ER doctors had suspected. She had a kidney stone. Now I've never had one, knock on wood, but I have heard they are about one of the most painful things you could possibly get. Diane was discharged from the hospital with pain medication and instructions. Apparently, she passed most of the stone in the hospital. Later, she was told the stone would pass completely.

A couple of days later, I received a call from our primary care physician's assistant. She said that Diane needed to get to the emergency room immediately because she had severe blockage. Without delay I informed Diane and again, we rushed to the hospital only this time, Diane was not in pain, but scared to death. What we did not realize at the time was that the physician's assistant was looking at a scan from *before* Diane had passed the kidney stone and she did not realize the blockage was in fact the stone. To the physician assistant, it just showed up as blockage. Thinking back, she probably acted appropriately. So after several more tests at the hospital confirmed no blockage, we went home with peace of mind.

This is where things get complicated. Have you ever experienced severe anxiety or panic attacks? I don't mean just nervousness or heart palpitations, but paralyzing anxiety attacks. I have not but my wife began to have them. She missed work and some of our children's activities. With the passing of time, she started missing more and more. I can't even begin to describe how this was having an impact on me. I could not stand to see my beautiful, energetic, sometimes crass wife, crippled on the couch because of this "disease." I use the term "disease" because I really didn't know at the time what we were up against. It wasn't until I researched anxiety that I came to find out there is more money spent on medication for anxiety and depression than for any other illness or disease in the world. Researchers believe that a significant traumatic event can be the trigger of chronic anxiety.

I cried a lot. She did too. I felt so helpless. I wanted to somehow make this go away for her. When I married her I made a vow to always take care of her. The sad reality was that I could not. There wasn't anything I could do to help her.

Diane was told she needed to go see a psychologist. They put her on anti-depressant medication; the happy medicine. The anxiety began to subside over a few months but Diane was still not herself. The medicine she was on was keeping her from having any feelings at all. She got to the point where she was indifferent about everything. In other words, she didn't care about anything. Diane functioned, but she didn't feel.

After a few sessions with a psychologist and several visits to her regular doctor, things were going to change. The psychologist said Diane needed to be on the medication for a year before she could be weaned off successfully. She used to come home laughing about her appointments with the psychologist. Diane hated the medicine but most off all she hated not being able to feel. She began going to see her regular doctor, who was not on our medical insurance plan. I didn't care one bit. I wanted my wife back. The kids wanted their mother back. Her sisters wanted their sister back. The neighbors wanted their friend back.

The long and short of this is that after some blood tests, it turned out my wife did not need to be on anti-depressant medication. What she needed was to be on medicine to correct her hypothyroidism. One of the leading symptoms of hypothyroidism is anxiety.

In retrospect that was probably the most difficult time in my life. I cried because I could not help her. I cried because our neighbors cried. I cried because our kids did not understand. Throughout this terrible ordeal, I learned to love my wife and children better. I also became more sensitive to the needs of others and treated them better. In the end, I was less selfish and had become a much better person.

****

The fourth life changing event for me and hopefully several other people is also the reason I decided to write this book. It is something that has given me the purpose I have been searching for. Aside from being a husband and parent, it defines me. It gives me strength. It gives me hope. It gives others strength. It gives others hope.

****

One of my favorite movies of all-time is *Field of Dreams*. It is one of the few that has brought tears to my eyes. The others are *Brian's Song*, *Rudy,* and *Backdraft*. All of these stories reflect my life in some way. *Brian's Song* is a classic example because it is a heart-wrenching true story of courage and fear. *Rudy* also struck a chord with me because of the number of times I had people tell me I could not accomplish something. I am especially fond of *Backdraft* because if I had it to do over again, I would have been a fireman. However, if I had to pick one above the others it would have to be *Field of Dreams*. The obvious father references in the movie really hit home with me. One particular quote from this extremely well-made movie comes to mind. Author Terrance Mann has finally seen the light with regards to Ray Kinsella's decision to destroy his farm and build a baseball field in its place.

> *"The one constant through all the years, Ray, has been baseball. America has rolled by like an army of steamrollers. It's been erased like a blackboard, rebuilt, and erased again. But, baseball has marked the time. This field, this*

game, is a part of our past, Ray. It reminds us of all that once was good, and could be again. Oh, people will come, Ray. People will most definitely come."

I think that *Field of Dreams* is a great example of how much impact baseball (or another escape) can have on one man's life. As we watch Ray come closer and closer to the goal of his surreal adventure, we also see some of ourselves in his easy to love, yet often hard to understand character. He is driven by the memory of a father whom he can no longer patch things up with, and determined to be a better man to his family. In the end, when he gets that second opportunity to play catch with his dad and discovers the reality of his relationship with him, we see what sets this movie apart from so many others.

Just like Ray Kinsella, I want another opportunity to play catch with my dad.

****

Sometimes the biggest risk you can take is not taking the risk at all.

The fourth life changing event that I am referring to was when I formed my business, Diamond Academy, Inc.

Chapter Eight

MEASURE OF SUCCESS

At Diamond Academy, we believe the keys to a successful sports and life experience are opportunities. Diamond Academy exists to provide athletes with these opportunities so they can excel both on and off the field in a controlled, structured environment. Okay ... that is what the mission statement says anyway. But what does that mean exactly?

I formed Diamond Academy in the fall of 2004, originally due to the high volume of requests I received to provide private baseball instruction. You may feel inclined to ask, what makes my business different from any other of a similar nature out there? I'm afraid I do not know the answer. What I do know is that I have done this for all the right reasons. What I do know is it has changed me more than you can imagine. In an earlier chapter I talk about sports being used as an escape. Well, this really applies to me. It's just that now I have the perfect opportunity to try to get my message across and have a forum to do it. The big catch here is that I get to use baseball or softball, two things I absolutely love, as my delivery mechanism.

One of the things that I aim to teach is what it means to be an athlete, just how truly special it is and things we can do to make not only the sports world, but our own world, a much better place to live. Statistics reveal that of all the kids playing youth baseball today, only 3 percent will play organized baseball after the age of fourteen. My take on this is that 100 percent of them will participate in the bigger league of life. That is the message that I hope to get across. I will continue to teach baseball or softball as long as there is a demand for it, but I really hope to be teaching much more than the basics of the game. It is far more important to me that the kids I teach are good kids and get good grades in school as it is that they hit the ball well.

Certain attributes define young athletes as they turn into young men and women. Some of these include the commitment to improvement, the will to win and the ability to learn from mistakes and be motivated by failure. Of course winning is sometimes important in sports, but what is even more crucial are the character building aspects that you can develop through sports.

The average career for a major league baseball position player is 5.6 years. One in five of every position player will have only a single-year career. What is just as disappointing is that at every point of his career, the player's chance of his career ending abruptly is at least 11 percent. The odds are tremendously stacked against a professional sports career but it is our job, as parents, coaches and instructors, to foster dreams as much as it is to keep things in perspective.

Another area in which we hope to educate students and parents about is steroid use among young athletes. In 2006, the Center for Disease Control (CDC) estimated that 6 percent of the high school population have or are using steroids. That's one million kids. It gets a whole lot worse. Furthermore, the CDC estimates that 11 to 12 percent of all high school junior and senior males have used the stuff to boost their performance.

While my business is not a huge money maker right now, I do believe there is huge potential, particularly if I franchised. *But that is not what this is about for me.* One of my very first customers had written me a check for $500. That is a significant amount of money to a brand new business. She had purchased a package of private lessons for her son. After seeing her son for the first two sessions, I realized that he did not want to be there. His parents wanted him to be there. I did not hesitate to return the money.

****

It's easy to get caught up in the crap that is life.

I once had to attend an off-site leadership conference. The speaker was a third party expert on career development. This was held in the corporate auditorium and the speaker was on the stage. Overall, there were about ninety people in attendance. One of the exercises involved closing your eyes and answering a series of questions. One of the questions asked was, how many people truly enjoy their profession and feel they have made the right career choice? Answers were to be given by a show of hands and the speaker was also a participant. The logical thing for me to do was to conform to the response that was expected. Those of you who know me ... well, you get the picture. After everyone decided whether or not to put their hand in the air, the speaker then instructed everyone to open their eyes. I could hardly believe my own eyes. Almost every single person in that room, everyone except for me and the speaker, had their hand in the air for the career question. At that very moment it hit me that this wasn't going to be good for me.

As I expected, the speaker singled me out. Keep in mind that I am in a room full of my peers, vice presidents, senior leaders, my boss and several other prominent corporate executives. The dialogue went something like this:

Speaker: "Steve, you realize that you are the only person in this room, other than me, who has not raised your hand?"

Me: "Yep."

Speaker: "And you realize that you are going to have to explain this and it very well may be the end of your career at this company?"

A medley of laughter was heard.

Me: "Yep."

More laughter.

Speaker: "Well, let's hear it."

Me: "You first. You had your hand down too."

Even more laughter.

Speaker: "Nice try. I don't work for this company."

Me: "Oh well, what the hell. I pretty much knew I would be one of the select few who would not raise their hand. I sure didn't expect to be the only one."

Speaker: "You weren't. I also did not raise my hand."

Me: "Conventional wisdom told me, 'put your hand up, fly under the radar, and keep your mouth shut.' But most people in this room who know me know that it would be outside my character to conform. So in all honesty, in order for me to explain this, I need to play a game."

Speaker: "By all means, join me on stage."

So I make my way toward the stage, climb up the stairs and take my place behind the podium. At last, my fifteen minutes of fame has arrived! After all these years, I finally have the golden opportunity to address Corporate America. The funny thing is that even though I was put under the spotlight in front of my superiors, the leaders of the company, and various other important people who could fire me on the spot, I wasn't the least bit nervous. I didn't realize it at the time, but somehow the opportunity I had long waited for had suddenly fallen on my lap. You better believe I was finally going to let people in.

Me: "Okay, so now I'm going to ask a similar question. Close your eyes. Now tell me, how many of you have a hobby?"

If I remember correctly, every hand in the room shot up in the air like an arrow. Before pressing on, I let them take a long, hard look.

Me: "Now, keep your hands up and close your eyes again. How many of you have ever gotten paid to perform your hobby?"

This time just a few hands stayed up. Again, I allowed them to look around.

Me: "Close your eyes one last time and put your hands down. Now, imagine being able to make a living doing your hobby. Last question, how many of you, if it were possible, would turn your hobby into your career?"

At this juncture, I instruct them to open their eyes. Now the 99 percent of the attendees in the room who previously answered that they had made the right career choice had dwindled down to less than 10 percent. Six people, to be exact, had their hand in the air.

Me: "So, now you see why my hand was not raised when asked if I felt I had made the right career choice. I do get paid to perform my hobby."

Just as I am about to leave the podium and exit the stage, the speaker chimes in.

Speaker: "You don't get off that easy. Let's hear about it."

After issuing a disclaimer that my hobby is not a conflict of interest and is not anything that affects my time or ability to perform my job at this company, I begin to elaborate.

Me: "I run a youth baseball and softball academy, outside of our business hours of course."

Speaker: "Very interesting. And is it successful enough for you to do full-time?"

Me: "It very easily could be, but the reality is that my clients are in school all day long."

Speaker: "And why is doing that much more rewarding than working here?"

Me: "That could turn into a pretty long discussion, but I'll be brief. I'll preface it by saying no offense to anyone in this room or this organization. This career has afforded me opportunities, and as strange as it seems, has driven me to find something that I can pour my heart and soul into. That does not mean I don't work hard at my current job. It also doesn't imply that I don't care about doing things to help this organization. I also do not hate my job by any means. But, I sit in these leadership meetings listening to people tell us how rewarding these careers can be and how fulfilling these jobs are. I really struggle with that. What is rewarding to me is when little Joey comes up to me, hugs me, and tells me he got two hits in a game and an A on his Science test. Sometimes seeing the joy on their sweet innocent faces brings tears to my eyes. I feel that I have played an integral role in their efforts. So, I reward them for their grades. Statistics show that less than 3 percent of youth athletes play sports beyond the age of fourteen. My thought is that 100 percent of them participate in the bigger game of life. While my delivery mechanism is instructing students in baseball or softball, my goal is hopefully that I am teaching them things they will use far beyond the baseball and softball field. I have an entire program structured around this. I teach them about respect and integrity and sportsmanship and ethics. I have e-mails written from grateful parents that will absolutely bring tears to your eyes. I give these kids confidence. I give them strength, but most of all I give them hope. In return, they give me strength. They give me hope."

Speaker: "Wow. You may step down."

I step down to applause from the audience. I'm happy to say that I didn't lose my job either.

****

Over the past few years I have come to realize something important. I've spent my whole life in a career because that is what is expected of us. That is what our society demands of us. The challenge for me is that I came to a point in my life where I felt I needed to make a difference in someone's life. I needed to have an impact on someone's life. I wanted to make people believe. Not only that, I longed to make people inspire other people to believe. After all this time, I now have the opportunity to do just that.

Oftentimes, we get so caught up in our daily lives that we forget there is more to life than our jobs, houses, cars and lifestyles. This thing I have created, this message that I have to share, has inspired me like nothing else ever has. It has made me a better person.

What will matter is not your success, but your significance and the impact you can have on others.

Is it working? Unfortunately, I do not really know the answer to this question because I have not fully defined what "it" is. But the one thing I can be sure of is that I have had an impact on some young lives, through baseball or softball. I also believe that some parents have changed their perspective regarding their children's sports lives. I think one of the long-term measures of my success will be how many players or students will remember me years from now. As for me, there is about a handful of baseball coaches that I remember throughout my life. I remember them not because we won championships or they let me play all of the good positions. My memory of them remains strong because of how they delivered their messages. They would make eye contact when speaking with you. Some of them would talk about character. One would say a prayer before each game asking the LORD to keep us free from injury. Most of the old school coaches commanded respect. They all enforced integrity and insisted that we exercise good sportsmanship. Above all they taught us about ethics.

But this is not a one way street. I challenge some of these kids at times in the hope that it will have a long-term effect on their lives. I challenge them with thought-provoking questions such as when it comes down to the wire, do they picture themselves succeeding? Are they ultimately afraid of being successful because then it would be expected of them? Do they have the desire and discipline to become all that they can be? Do they have the confidence and optimism required to become a leader? Again, these questions may seem sports related because of the forum that I am asking them in, but every single one of them pertains to life.

A short-term measure I use to gauge my impact is how many of the players or students that I coach come back to play the following year. So far, things look pretty good. While the testimonials below are for the most part related to baseball, I would like to think that the impact will reach beyond the perimeter of a sports field. The reason for that is that in my programs, a young athlete does not progress from one stage to another without applying the same or more effort in the classroom as on the field. That is something tangible I can measure.

"Steve ... Tyler loved the lessons but it was my husband John who raved about you ... I am not talking about just saying, yeah, it was good. He RAVED about you. He LOVED the way you taught, loved your philosophy, and loved how you interacted with Tyler."

~ MB

"I wanted to thank you. Steve, you did a great job in helping my son Chris improve his hitting. You've also taught him about sportsmanship and hard work. Thanks again for the one-on-one training you provided Chris and thanks for a Grand Slam of a baseball training program."

~ MR

"WOW! Montana had a great day! Two doubles ... solid hits to the outfield. When Montana was pitching, she was the talk of the baseball complex. We had the biggest on looking crowd. Everyone wanted to see this girl who is striking out these boys ... I just wanted to thank you again for having such a passion and sharing it with others. I cannot express thanks to you enough for the training and future training that she will get from you. As a girl playing in a boy dominated sport she had several obstacles to climb. You made it possible for her to climb this hill and compete at the same level. This will go far beyond baseball. Again, thank you."

~ GM

"Steve ... I can't thank you enough for the effort you have put forth with Dominic this winter. Your approach and expertise have made and will continue to make a huge impact. All he talks about now is baseball, baseball, baseball ... after his homework is done of course. But it is his overall confidence in EVERYTHING that has gone through the roof!"

~ LL

For more testimonials, please visit our web site at http://www.diamond-academy.com/testimonials.htm

Chapter Nine

I NEED A HERO

Growing up, I don't think I ever really had a hero, per se, but there have been some people that I've looked up to. Many individuals today consider their mother or father to be their hero. In my case, I wouldn't classify either of them as such. That does not mean I didn't love them dearly. To me, a hero is a term that I never fully understood. On the surface, I thought a hero was someone who saved other people. Many people, particularly children, list athletes as their hero. Personally, I don't think athletes deserved to be praised as heroes. They are getting paid millions of dollars simply to play a game. I have no problem with kids looking up to athletes or having them as role models, but they are a far cry from being true heroes. What really bothers me is that a good number of these star players don't behave like a role model should. Then there are those who could not possibly be further from being a role model, yet today's media insists that they are worthy of this distinction. The media has the power to turn ordinary people into a bona fide hero and that really scares me.

There certainly are true heroes out there. Look no further than the events of September 11th, 2001. How about the people who went into burning buildings knowing full well that they might not make it out alive, or the people who stormed the cockpit of United Flight 93, or the people who risked their health and psychological wellbeing cleaning up in the aftermath of the destruction at the World Trade Center? Those people are heroes. And what about the people who have to live through the horror of continuing the rest of their lives without someone they lost in the tragic events of that day? Those people are heroes.

When I reflect back to the days my mother spent in the hospital before she passed away, one of the first things that pops into my head is just how special the people providing Hospice Care are. These people are my heroes. The information below comes from a World Health Organization report.

****

The World Health Organization (WHO) defined palliative care as "the active total care of patients whose disease is not responsive to curative treatment." This definition stresses the terminal nature of the disease. However, the term can also be used more generally to refer to anything that alleviates symptoms, even if there is also hope of a cure by other means; thus, a more recent WHO statement calls palliative care "an approach that improves the quality of life of patients and their families facing the problems associated with life-threatening illness." In some cases, palliative treatments may be used to alleviate the side effects of curative treatments, such as relieving the nausea associated with chemotherapy.

****

To me, "Saint" might be a much better title for these wonderful, self-sacrificing people who practice palliative care. Day in and day out, they are forced to look at death straight in the eye. On a daily basis, they somehow find ways to not only get themselves through the day, but others through the most difficult times in their lives. I can't even begin to imagine where they find the strength to do this every day.

If you were to ask any youth athlete today who their hero is, I would bet that many would spout out the name of a high-profile professional athlete. Baseball is our national pastime and the men who play it are too important to the fabric of America to trivialize, however, that does not mean we should put these athletes high on a pedestal. We have to make sure our children look up to these athletes to a certain point, but ultimately it is our job to help them understand where they should fall on the proverbial hero food chain, if you will. At the same time, we need to understand that these athletes do sometimes give our children the drive and passion to become all that they can be.

A hero is someone endowed with great courage and strength. You are your children's hero.

Please do not underestimate the significance of this statement. In your children's eyes, you are faster than a speeding bullet. You are more powerful than a locomotive. You are able to leap tall buildings in a single bound. Well, at least we all start out as heroes to our children. But one parental slip up and we can easily be stripped of that title.

I'm certainly not the best parent in the world. I am also not writing a book on parenting here. But what I am trying to do is instill in each of us some very simple thoughts that can help us become better human beings.

I still yell at my kids, but hopefully less than I used to. I'm still hard on them but only because they have such great potential. The more experience I gain as a parent, the better I listen to them. I hope I am open-minded enough to do so objectively. I also hope I am fair with them. Encouraging them more is something I definitely need to work on.

I honestly do not recall ANYONE ever telling me "I am proud of you," or "I believe in you." These words carry a tremendous amount of impact. If you believe in someone, they will begin to believe in themselves. You can encourage them to picture themselves being successful. I have spoken these words often over the past couple of years. One of the keys to getting any message across to the youth of today is by establishing and maintaining direct eye contact. They will feel the impact.

Every once in a while I will catch this special look in my son's or daughter's eyes. If you're a parent, you know the look I am talking about. It is a look of hope, a look of love, a look of devotion. Sometimes it is a look of fear, sorrow or anguish. But it is the kind of look that delivers this heart-tugging-hug when there is no physical contact. It's a look that sometimes brings tears to your eyes when you're alone and you think about it. It's this look that screams all of your child's hopes and dreams need to be encouraged and nurtured. It is this look that says, "You're my hero."

Earlier, I mentioned how my cheap plastic baseball trophies had somehow survived the fire in my mother and stepfather's house back in 1996. After all this time, I don't know how this could have possibly happened? Plastic melts quickly, after all. I said at the time that it was pretty ironic. Now I'm not so sure if it was irony or divine intervention that has put me in the direction that I am ultimately heading. I have often asked myself, am I now running this youth organization by choice or because it is what I was put on this planet to do? Maybe it's a little of both.

Although I'm glad they survived the fire, I do not have these trophies displayed in my house. In fact, they sit in a box in my garage. My kids have seen them and sometimes ask questions about them. The trophies sit in a box in the garage for a reason. You see, I had some pretty significant awards back in the day. These trophies were more than just participation awards which are given to all children today who participate in sports. I had won Most Valuable Player awards. I had won Championship trophies. I had won Sportsmanship awards. I had all of the awards that many of today's parents want their children to win. I happened to have a gift, particularly in baseball.

Yes, I am quite proud of what I have achieved. That is precisely why I do not display my awards in my house. I do not want *that* person to be the hero my children look up to. I do not want my children to strive for excellence simply because their dad did once upon a time. I want them to strive for excellence, both on and off the field, because of the values that have been instilled in them. While I want them to pursue excellence more off the field than on, I firmly believe that a large part of it begins on the field because that is where it is more fun.

When the time comes, and that may not be too far off as my children are eleven and thirteen, I will take out the trophies. I will even ask my kids to help me clean them up. I will encourage them to ask questions about them, although I'm quite sure they won't need the encouragement. And we will have a heart-to-heart conversation about all the reasons that I am who I am.

Realize that the little things ARE the things that matter.

I have, without a doubt, gotten better at keeping things in perspective over the last few years. This has been one of the toughest adjustments for me. I am as competitive as they come, *when I'm playing*. What I have learned though is how to focus my mind to keep things in perspective. I have also gotten much better at picking and choosing my battles, particularly when it comes to my children.

We all have moments where we see something on television or at a sporting event and we think to ourselves, how could that person have acted like that? In this day and age, youth sports are filled with parents who just don't get it. I'm not even trying right now and I can think of at least five stories of violence occurring at a youth sporting event. These unfortunate events are the reasons that coaches need to get certified and watch videos of how to handle adverse situations with parents. It is an awareness thing.

****

While my son was playing youth football, I witnessed something that I will never forget. He was eight years old at the time. I was one of the coaches on his team.

At that age, the coaches are allowed on the field to help the boys call plays and provide some direction. In this particular game, we were playing a team from one of our rival towns in a playoff game. This team we were playing against was from a larger town and their league had far more players than ours. Basically this meant they had a much larger pool of talented kids to pick from to form their top team. Without a doubt, we were overmatched.

At the time of this particular incident, we were losing 7-0. We could not move the football against the bigger, faster team. Out of desperation, I dug into our playbook and called a center sneak. This is a play that you rarely, if ever, see beyond the youth level. Basically, the quarterback gets the snap and places the ball on the ground right next to the center's foot. The entire team, except for the center, runs to one side of the field just like a sweep play. As that happens, especially with younger kids, the defense follows suit and chases the play in that direction. Only the play is not going that direction. The center picks up the ball and runs the opposite way.

Our play worked like a charm. Our center ran up the left side of the field for the game tying touchdown. One of the cornerbacks on defense who was originally playing on that left side had bought into our sweep right and was hustling as best as he could to get back to the left side and save the touchdown. We had kept our left side wide receiver around the middle of the field just in case he needed to block a defender who might be in position to make a tackle. As the cornerback was approaching our center for a tackle, our wide receiver threw one of the greatest blocks I have ever seen at this level. He flat-out laid the cornerback out on his back, allowing our center to score.

The cornerback had the wind knocked out of him pretty bad. The defensive coach on the field for the other team walked right past the kid as he was crying on the ground. I attended to the injured player and called over to the opposing coach to come and help him as he was really struggling to catch his breath. To my total astonishment, the coach got right in my face, pointed his finger at me and said, "I know his level of tolerance for pain!" I could not believe what I had just heard. All this coach cared about was that his cornerback blew his assignment and did not cover his area of the field, thus resulting in our touchdown. He was an eight year old kid! I heard a year or two later that this coach had been kicked out of coaching, as well he should have been.

****

We all want what is best for our children. To some, that might mean the most elite schools. For others, it could be the most coveted positions on the field. But to the majority of us, it just means we want our children to grow up to be, as we used to say back in the day, "good people." When all is said and done, what is it that really matters?

****

There are certain things I have read or watched over the past several years that have had such a profound impact on me that I simply must share them with others. Regardless if you are a sports fan or not, if you had the good fortune of hearing the speech Jim

Valvano gave during a televised sports award ceremony some years ago, I'm sure it made you teary-eyed. Jim Valvano was a very successful long-time college basketball coach and broadcaster. Jimmy V, as he came to be known, was diagnosed with cancer in June of 1992. At the 1993 ESPY Awards show broadcast by ESPN, Coach Valvano was presented with the Arthur Ashe Courage Award. His speech is something that I will never forget. I have not included the entire speech here but you can access it through The V Foundation web site at www.jimmyv.org. The following text will probably not have the same degree of impact on you as it had on me, but I sincerely hope it contains some things that you will give some deep thought to.

"I can't tell you what an honor it is to even be mentioned in the same breath with Arthur Ashe. This is something I certainly will treasure forever. But, as it was said on the tape, and I also don't have one of those things going with the cue cards, so I'm going to speak longer than anybody else has spoken tonight. That's the way it goes. Time is very precious to me. I don't know how much I have left, and I have some

things that I would like to say. Hopefully, at the end, I'll have something that will be important to other people too."

"But, I can't help it. Now, I'm fighting cancer; everybody knows that. People ask me all the time about how you go through your life and how is your day, and nothing is changed for me. As Dick said, I'm a very emotional, passionate man. I can't help it. That's being the son of Rocco and Angelina Valvano. It comes with the territory. We hug, we kiss, we love. And when people say to me how do you get through life or each day, it's the same thing. To me, there are three things we all should do every day. We should do this every day of our lives. Number one is laugh. You should laugh every day. Number two is think. You should spend some time in thought. And number three is, you should have your emotions moved to tears, could be happiness or joy. But think about it. If you laugh, you think, and you cry, that's a full day. That's a heck of a day. You do that seven days a week, you're going to have something special."

"... I always have to think about what's important in life to me are these three things. Where you started; where you are; and where you're gonna be. Those are the three things that I try and do every day."

"... I just got one last thing, I urge all of you, all of you, to enjoy your life, the precious moments you have. To spend each day with some laughter and some thought, to get your emotions going. To be enthusiastic every day and [as] Ralph Waldo Emerson said, "Nothing great could be accomplished without enthusiasm" -- to keep your dreams alive in spite of whatever problems you have. The ability to be able to work hard for your dreams to come true, to become a reality."

Jim Valvano

****

"Someday, it will all come to an end. There will be no more deadlines or sunrises or sunsets. Everything you have bought, earned or collected will pass to someone else. Your wealth, your fame and your power will become irrelevant. It will not matter what you owned. Your anger, frustrations, grudges and jealousies will disappear. Your hopes, dreams, plans and honey-do lists will expire. The wins and losses that once seemed so important will now become insignificant."

"What will matter is not what you bought, but what you built; not what you got, but what you gave. What will matter is not your success, but your significance. What will matter is not what you learned, but what you taught. What will matter is how you encouraged others. What will matter are not your memories, but the memories that live in those who loved you. What will matter is how long you will be remembered, by whom and for what."

Author, unknown

****

In my life over the past few years, the perspective I have gained from my four life changing events has made me flat out enjoy life better. It does not matter to me anymore what position my son or daughter plays in a game or whether they had to sit out for two innings. It does not matter to me anymore if they do not get a hit in a game or strike out or make an error or miss a free throw at the end of a game. Sure, I still discuss these things with my kids. But what does matter to me is, did my child encourage one of his team members when he or she struck out? What matters to me is that my kids try their best, no matter what activity they are doing. Do my kids say please and thank you? That matters. Do they hold their head up high in defeat? Do my children remain humble when they triumph over others? These things matter more than you know. Do my kids listen to their teachers? Do they listen to their coaches? Do they listen to their parents? Do they respect people? Once again, these things matter. It matters to me that my children treat people properly.

Without a doubt, caring about something that doesn't matter is much easier than caring about things that truly do matter. Caring about the things that we should care about takes far more energy than caring about things that are ultimately insignificant.

This all reminds me of a story I once read in a baseball magazine. It is a story about all that is good. It is a story about kids making a difference.

****

At a fundraising dinner for a school that serves children with learning disabilities, the father of one of the students delivered a speech that would never be forgotten by all who attended. After extolling the school and its dedicated staff, he posed a question.

“Everything God does is done with perfection. Yet, my son, Shay, cannot understand things as other children do. Where is God's plan reflected in my son?"

The audience was stilled by the query. The father continued. "I believe," the father answered, "that when God brings a child like Shay into the world, an opportunity to realize the Divine Plan presents itself. And it comes in the way people treat that child."

Then, he told the following story:

Shay and his father had walked past a park where some boys Shay knew were playing baseball. Shay asked, "Do you think they will let me play?" His father knew that most boys would not want him on their team. But the father also understood that if his son were allowed to play it would give him a much-needed sense of belonging.

Shay's father approached one of the boys on the field and asked if his son could play. The boy looked to his teammates for guidance. Receiving none, he took matters into his own hands and said, "We are losing by six runs, and the game is in the eighth inning. I guess he can be on our team and we'll try to put him up to bat in the ninth inning." In the bottom of the eighth inning, Shay's team scored a few runs but was still behind by three.

At the top of the ninth inning, Shay put on a baseball mitt and played in the outfield. Although no hits came his way, he was obviously ecstatic just to be on the field, grinning from ear to ear as his father waved to him from the stands.

In the bottom of the ninth inning, Shay's team scored again. Now, with two outs and bases loaded, the potential winning run was on base. Shay was scheduled to be the next batter. Would the team actually let Shay bat at this juncture and give away their chance to win the game?

Surprisingly, Shay was given the bat. Everyone knew that a hit was all but impossible because Shay didn't even know how to hold the bat properly, much less connect with the ball. However, as Shay stepped up to the plate, the pitcher moved a few steps to lob the ball in softly so Shay could at least be able to make contact. The first pitch came and Shay swung clumsily and missed. The look on his face was precious.

The pitcher again took a few steps forward to toss the ball softly toward Shay. As the pitch came in, Shay swung at the ball and hit a slow ground ball to the pitcher. The pitcher picked up the soft grounder and could easily have thrown the ball to the first baseman. Shay would have been out and that would have ended the game.

Instead, the pitcher took the ball and threw it on a high arc to right field, far beyond reach of the first baseman. Everyone started yelling, "Shay, run to first. Run to first." Never in his life had Shay ever made it to first base. He scampered down the baseline, wide-eyed and startled. Everyone yelled, "Run to second, run to second!" By the time Shay was rounding first base, the right fielder had the ball. He could have thrown the ball to the second baseman for a tag. But the right fielder understood what the pitcher's intentions had been, so he threw the ball high and far over the third baseman's head. Shay ran toward second base as the runners ahead of him deliriously circled the bases toward home. As Shay reached second base, the opposing shortstop ran to him, turned him in the direction of third base, and shouted, "Run to third!" As Shay rounded third, the boys from both teams were screaming, "Shay, run home!" Shay ran home, stepped on home plate and was cheered as the hero for hitting a "grand slam" and winning the game for his team.

"That day," said the father softly with tears now rolling down his face, "the boys from both teams helped bring a piece of the Divine Plan into this world."

****

Living a life that matters does not happen by accident. It's not a matter of circumstance but of choice. Choose to live a life that matters.

We end our prayers each night with the following:

"... and God please give us the strength to love, care for and respect others. Amen."

Chapter Ten

I'M SCARED

One of the things I believe will be most difficult for me to accept will be my kids growing up. I'm not talking about them becoming adults. I guess I am more concerned about their upcoming teen years, the driving, going away to college, and all the other things they will encounter through early adulthood. How do I know they will make the right choices in life? They will certainly face many challenges and pressures throughout their lifetime and so many of those will be different from those that I faced. I hope that I have prepared them properly.

Pressure can mean so many different things to people. For youngsters, they may feel pressure as the expectation to be successful in school or sports. For adults, the expectations of high performance in their job can create pressure. To me, there is no greater pressure than being a parent.

This is something all parents have to go through at some point in their lives. The real challenge lies in figuring out how to make sure the morals and values we teach our children far outweigh the negative outside influences they will encounter in their lifetime. These outside influences are changing faster than we can keep up so the task becomes all that more daunting for us. Oftentimes, we don't even find out what these influences are until it's too late. We have to stay informed as parents and remain friends with our children. No matter how hard it may be at times, we have to talk to them. More importantly, we must listen to them. Unfortunately, I did not have the good fortune of having my parents help me with tough decisions growing up. But what I did have in my favor were the good values that were instilled in me before having to face these decisions.

There are an endless number of things we can do to help our children make the right choices in life. But even with our guidance and support, they will occasionally make the wrong choices. This is a hard cold fact. So it is our job as parents to partner up with our children. Partner? With my child? Yes, form a partnership with your child. By definition, a partnership is a cooperative relationship between people or groups who agree to share responsibility for achieving some specific goal. A partnership entails more than just having the soft skills to communicate with our children. It is a journey that takes time and hard work. It is built on a foundation of trust and credibility. It is unconditional love.

In my opinion, trust is probably the most crucial element of successful relationships. The word trust implies instinctive, unquestioning belief in and reliance upon something. It is a firm reliance on the integrity, ability, or character of a person or thing. I ask all of my students for their definition of the word trust. Invariably, they all have a pretty solid understanding of what the word means. As their baseball instructor, it is important that they trust me. I always tell them that their definition is the same as mine because it is. But I also tell them that I am going to add something to the end of the definition and that is "with the same goal in mind." I go on to explain that I realize they are coming to me to get better at a particular skill. I then remind them that they need to trust me because I have that same goal in mind as they do. I think they get it. Is it any different in our own relationships with our children? I hope that my chidren trust me.

When I speak of outside influences, however, I am not just referring to the obvious; drugs, alcohol, smoking. I am especially concerned about influences that did not exist when I was growing up. One of the biggest concerns I have is the all mighty Internet.

I have been involved in technology my whole adult life. I was part of the entire Internet revolution and the dot-com boom of the late 90's. The "dot-com bubble" was a speculative one covering roughly 1995-2001 during which stock markets in Western nations saw their value increase rapidly from growth in the new Internet sector and related fields. The period was marked by the founding (and in many cases, spectacular failure) of a group of new Internet-based companies commonly referred to as dot-coms. A combination of rapidly increasing stock prices, individual speculation in stocks, and widely available venture capital funding created a ridiculous environment in which many of these businesses dismissed standard business models, focusing on increasing their market share at the expense of the bottom line. The bursting of the dot-com bubble marked the beginning of a relatively mild, yet rather lengthy recession in Western nations.

Many, many people profited from the dot-com era though, including me. It became relatively easy to make money purchasing stocks. When a new company, particularly a technology company with promise was about to go public, it was not uncommon for people to purchase and sell that stock the same day. I did it. Others did it. And we did it paying incredibly high prices for these stocks but it didn't matter because we knew that by the end of the day, the price would soar even higher.

I am not saying that this period of time was all that bad. People made millions of dollars. People began to realize that you could make money on the Internet. Thousands of legitimate businesses began to and still do make millions and millions of dollars on the Internet.

Thousands and thousands of morally questionable businesses make the same money. It is estimated as of this writing that pornography makes up nearly one fourth of all Internet sites. In 2005, Google™, the world's most popular search engine, returned over 35 million web pages when you search for the word "porn." It had almost a billion web pages catalogued that contained the word "porn." An estimated $57 billion dollars is spent annually on Internet pornography. It is calculated that child pornography generated more than $3 billion annually. These eye-opening statistics really scare me. Porn revenue is larger than the combined revenues of all professional baseball, football, and basketball teams.

Getting back to child pornography statistics, what does that mean to us as parents? For one thing, it means that we better educate ourselves about technology and our children. We better know how to secure our home computers. With all of the other things we have going on in our lives, we must take time to pay close attention to additional things that could prove to be potentially harmful to our children.

There are plenty of other things we need to be aware of in regard to protecting ourselves and our children. Internet chat rooms and blogging sites are two more. Chat rooms allow virtually anyone with an Internet connection to chat with someone else who also has an Internet connection via a keyboard. The scariest part of this is that while your identity COULD BE protected, oftentimes it is not. But it also means that while your child thinks he or she is chatting with another boy or girl their own age who lives in another state or country, the reality could be that your child is really chatting with a fifty-year-old man who practically lives next door or a twenty-year-old man who lives two states away. There is absolutely no way to know for sure.

A blog, on the other hand, is defined as a user generated web site where entries are made in journal style and displayed in a reverse chronological order.

Blogs often provide commentary or news on a particular subject, such as food, politics, or local news; some function as more personal online diaries. A typical blog combines text, images and links to blogs, web pages and other media related to its topic. The ability for readers to leave comments in an interactive format is an important part of many blogs. Most blogs are primarily textual although some focus on photographs, sketches, videos or audio and are a part of a wider network of social media. The term "blog" is derived from "Web log." Blogging is the act of maintaining or adding content to a blog. But there is often a lack of control to what can be posted on a blog and that is a growing concern.

So what can we do about it? Before we can inform others about these dangers, first we must educate ourselves and those closest to us. It makes perfect sense to start by educating our children. Luckily for us, there are good-hearted educators we can probably talk to who might be willing to help. Listening attentively to our children and praying wouldn't hurt either.

Our society, while it probably isn't all that different from years ago, now seems like a very scary place. When I was a kid, I used to be able to leave my house at 8:00 in the morning and come home when the street lights came on. Even then we could still play outside in the dark on our own block. Things in the twenty-first century have changed drastically. Unfortunately, we cannot allow our children the same freedom anymore and there are a number of reasons for this. The Federal Bureau of Investigation (FBI) stated in 2005 that as of 1982, child abduction had increased 444 percent. Although it may seem like it, this is not a typo. Four hundred and forty-four percent! About half of the abductions were children between the ages of four and eleven. More than 70 percent of the abductions were girls.

I am not a religious man by any means but I do believe in God. I may not go to church every Sunday but I do pray. My children attend a Catholic school. Yet, there are plenty of times that I question why certain things happen. We all do. From time to time, certain things do make us question our faith.

I often wonder why I have been without a father for so long. I also wonder why I will probably live more than half of my life without any parents at all. I question why someone would fly airplanes into buildings, killing thousands of people. I ask myself why any adult would ever harm an innocent child. For that matter, I wonder why any human being would ever harm another human being. I wonder why I am losing friends and relatives prematurely. I wonder why some of my friends have lost a child. It obviously is all just part of life and we all must learn to face the challenges that will cause us to question our faith head-on.

All in all, I think one of the most significant things I have learned throughout the years is that life is sometimes not fair. That must be true. My children tell me so. It's not fair if one of my kids gets ice cream when the other one wasn't around. It's not fair that one has to do more chores one week because they procrastinated the first time around. "Not fair, not fair, not fair," is something my children say a great deal. If you are a parent, too, I'm sure you've also heard this quote quite often.

But it is how we deal with all of life's situations that can make us better people. For me, the key is to keep the particular situation in the right perspective. That is far easier for adults to do than it is for children. But at the same time, that is where we can really teach. Our kids will want no part of our rationale. But I do believe their conscience does hear our message. It's the things like this that *can* make a difference.

Chapter Eleven

OUR PART

As I mentioned often throughout the book, we play a massive role in the lives of today's children. Whether we are a parent, teacher, coach, or for that matter just someone who a child might look up to, we have a responsibility to our youth. We cannot possibly expect children to lead by example if the example we are leading by is not a good one. From an athletic standpoint, we need to send a message that extends beyond the field. As parents, we have to stay involved. Our teachers must remain aware. We must continually educate ourselves about today's youth.

I am not a writer (I'm sure you had trouble figuring that one out), but I thought I owed it to myself to share the thoughts I have expressed in this book. It has helped me tremendously. Hopefully at least one person who has made it to the end of the book has come away with a slightly different perspective on some of the topics that were addressed.

If you are a parent, I hope this book made you think about some of the little things that matter. If you're a coach, I hope that you encourage your players more and give them opportunities to be successful. If you're a student, apply yourself. We believe in you. And lastly, if you are an athlete, may you give more effort, win with dignity, hold your head up high in defeat and develop yourself into a wonderful human being. More importantly than all of that, be a good student and a good kid.

I don't know what it is anymore that drives me other than my family. But I do hope that after all is said and done, I am a better person. I hope that when my time has passed, people will stop and say, "Steve was a good guy."

In no particular order, on the following page are some closing thoughts that I consider significant and would like to share. I keep a printed copy of them in two places knowing that every day I will be in one of those two places.

- Be nice to people.
- Realize that the little things do matter.
- Take time to hug the kids every day and tell the people you care about that you love them.
- Your success will not matter, but your significance and the impact that you can have on others will.
- Learn to deal with life's disappointments ... there will be many.
- It's okay to cry.
- It takes years to build trust and only seconds to destroy it.
- A hero is someone endowed with great courage and strength. Continue to be your children's hero.
- Encourage our children ... and remember that they are just children.
- Sometimes, the biggest risk you can take is not taking the risk at all.
- Perception is often reality.

… and lastly, I've learned that *you'll never stand taller than when you stoop to help a child.*

Made in the USA
Middletown, DE
24 September 2023

39223661R00084